for Beatrice Byrd,
June Rocheteau,
& Glenna LaCouture

Past. (Tense)

Present. (Tense)

Future. (Perfect)

Whose Clock?

ACKNOWLEDGMENTS

I offer my deepest gratitude and love to Fatimah Asghar, Danez Smith, Mckendy Fils-Aime, Aaron Samuels, Franny Choi, Sean P. Mulroy, Charif Shanahan, Sean DesVignes, Rachel McKibbens, Shira Erlichman, Jared Paul, Cave Canem/Bread Loaf Sicily/FAWC/ Callaloo faculty and workshop groups, Lynne Procope & Thomas Sayers Ellis for really good ideas, Maya Marshall, Airea D. Matthews, Wolfie E. Rawk, Jerrica Park, Khury Petersen-Smith, Emerson Brisbon, Elliott Fukui, Corina McCarthy-Fadel for all your assistance in the writing & the living, and to Write A House for the sanctuary to do the work.

"The First Time I Was Black" first appeared in *Union Station*. "Two Byrds" first appeared on *Poets.org*. "Skkkrmble 4 Africa" first appeared in *Perigee*. "Topsy (direct)" first appeared in *heART Online*. "Disposition: Criminal" first appeared in *Winter Tangerine*. "Illegal" and "Your Heart Is a Swollen Witch" first appeared in *Black Heart*. "Sun Ra Speaks to Gucci Mane" first appeared in *Kinfolks Quarterly*. "Unfinished Letters From the Most Popular Kid in the Psych Ward" first appeared in *The Offing*. "Epigenetics" first appeared in *Muzzle* under the title "As Around the Sun the Earth Knows She's Revolving."

INTRODUCTION

This book of poems is intended as a game that grows outward. The idea is to reinvent the dozens and juke what is truly oppressive about the world in which we live. *The Dozen* is also literal: 12 poems in each section, playing off of each other, scraping against each other messily, harmonizing, clowning each other and sometimes themselves. Above all, *The Dozen* is intended as an invitation to unwind the clocks, shake off the shame we learned as kids, stop talking about other people's mamas, and call out the things in our culture that are so ugly they turned Medusa to stone.

PAST. (TENSE)

TOPSY (ALTERNATING)

Some people would have you believe
Thomas Edison killed the elephant Topsy
as a public spectacle during the War of Currents.
He was not present for the killing, the viewing,
but some would blame Prometheus
for Philly in '85, Detroit in '67.

Topsy was stolen from her mother, smuggled
and billed as the exceptional American-born
elephant. Then, she was wicked,
they said, trampling the neck of a patron in St. Paul.
They sold her to a whiskeyblind overseer
at Luna Park who fed her a lit cigarette
and forced her to haul a rocketship
down Coney's boardwalk, steeplechase
to the moon, dazzling the gawking
sunbathers with her penitence
like a pickaninny at auction.

Her restless legs had no love for
a savior she did not ask for.
I have been a disappointment to many men
in the same way. Stomping roughshod.
The heart wants what the brain
                    thinks it deserves.

She killed the vicious handler.
The park wanted to lynch her, as a moral thing.

Deemed inhumane,
they poisoned her first;
the current finished the job,
and Edison's company made snuff,
sold 15,000 tickets, barked *Step right up folks!*
Witness the magnificent, the phantastic
        spectre of a petulant exotic beast!
        Come unhinge your maw and feast.

13

The First Time I Was Black

I was staring out the sliding glass door
at the mourning doves in the backyard.
My white mother came up
behind me and said that if anyone
didn't want to be my friend at school
it was their loss. I asked,
Why would anyone not want to be my friend?

well,
because you're black.

I looked at my hands
uncomprehending.

It only took until nine years old
to fully understand her riddle.

There was no family Christmas
that year for fear my neo-Nazi uncle,
newly out of jail, would massacre
his sisters' swamp-blooded children
and his sisters who had transgressed
and their lovers who were born.

When the police discovered him, he flung
his AK-47 into Hyannis Harbor, and
when he returned after another bid,
I learned the recurring embrace of a
family which forgives all the wrong things.

As I grew, it was clear that
bodies not built for waltzes
were the only ones
that would catch
and hold me.

My inheritance—emulation
of unconditional reluctance
to give up.

I did not renounce my name
but chose genocide's ashtray,

to run
into the black,
into what they'd
named me.

A GUIDED MEDITATION

Give your hands up
to this moment.
Imagine a barbecue—
children running freely,
magnolia on the wind.
It's 1880, you're in a crowd.
Despite the tranquility,
they're screaming.

You shift your weight, anxious,
watching dark flesh torn open.
They want pieces of him:
Fingers. Chunks of meat. His dick.
All you know is this heat stench,
this agreement, unfiring synapse.

Thank grace for every moment
you don't acknowledge the past:
As you water the aloe plant, you are
unburdened by the cough of slave ships.

Now imagine reading these words
without your brother's body in the park
or the bullethole mind so impressed
by friction.

Let's say privilege doesn't exist.
Your father isn't locked up on drug charges.
No one asks what your skin means
or makes you cry in a native tongue.
Your miseducation shows
through the holes in your sweater.

Pretend you know nothing about Phillis Wheatley,
the Protestants, Delta Creole, Manifest Destiny,
Benjamin Kiteflyer Electric, the Bible,
Atticus Finch, the blues, the Seminole,
or your heart, your heart—
pretend it is not small or easily distracted
so that you might love without bursting to tears, yes.

Love now the hair follicles on your belly,
and the place in your mind unoccupied
by fear of your government or neighborhood.

Love that you already won
with your skin, your balls,
your father's wallet or your own.
Love your luck, your mother,
your hometown, love that you
have not starved to death.

This is not an indictment;
guilt is as useless as a slaveowner's child.
Your life is a calm field.
The earth below it is caked with blood.

Now imagine me,
hand outstretched,
in spite of your ugly
textbooks and amnesia.

Love less your white pockets,
love more your ears, equipped
with silence, and your G-d mechanic
mind for its ability to change,
and give up your hands.

Split the globe open and look
where we can push
this cinder block of brutality.

How different our fathers' eyes are.

Every bigot-tongue still swinging
is one step closer to caging you.

Imagine waking up tomorrow
to find these words under your skin.

[HAUNTS]

You see, de white folks don't git in de spirit. Dey don't shout, pray, hum, an' sing all through de services lak us do. Dey don't believe in a heap o' things us niggers knows 'bout. Dey tells us dey ain't no ghos', but us knows better n dat. I's seed ghos' an haints [haunts] all my life. I's seed 'em right here on dis gallery where I's a-settin'.

— Minerva Grubbs, former slave, in a WPA interview.

I. In the morning
they cut out her tongue,
buried it in a paper box,
and tore the skin
from the belly
of her drum.
This seer bled
and lived to tell.

When they unearthed
the fleshy muscle again,
how it wriggled like a botfly,
how it transcended
white gravity.

She, Oracle of Defy,
knew Godbuzz
as invocation, a beacon
to Hades' expatriates,
a call without response,
save for a vision.

As the scribe
dipped the tip of what
once rested on the dirt floor
of her mouth in his inkwell
he could never know the living
the way the dead know us.

II.   I do not fear becoming illegible,
only mute, fixed in the past.

It was Providence,
a sublet in servants' quarters.
The faucet would erupt
like an unexpected wound.
The bathroom light turned
on and off by some unseen hand.

Downstairs in the dark one night,
the swollen witch in my chest
beckoned me to the kitchen.

A greenish figure bent over
the stove, shrouded in pearl silence.

My eyes unquestioning,
I stared back, still liquid
and breathing. Flinching

in an unspoken language
with all that refuses death.

Your Heart Is a Swollen Witch
(Never Forget, 1692)

Satan set his hot feet to the good Earth.
In the end, twenty five hanged for having fits
or slowing the thrash of bodies.
Men fed dogs witch cakes—urine and rye—
to determine guilt, as if it were the body of Christ.

God's love shone in the rotting teeth of masters.
Parris, trembling under the hammer of witches,
beat Tituba, his slave, until her tongue slipped
into hell's mouth. The men who owned
made their fear a practice.

The tryals laid the brick of asylums,
sang electric shock therapy,
axed the Black Dahlia,
let Cosby drug a city—

Salem is a water-logged corpse
floating in America's chest,
law books filled with
child-sized nooses.

A mighty coven gathers
under the red moon
to cast it into the jagged sea.

Two

April 7, 1709
I rose before 6 o'clock
and read two chapters
in Hebrew and 250 verses
in Homer's *Odyssey*
and made an end of it.
I said my prayers devoutly.
I ate milk for breakfast.
I danced my dance.
The men began to work
this day to dig for brick.
I settled my accounts
and read Italian.
I reproached my wife.

September 3, 1709
I ate roast chicken for dinner.
In the afternoon I beat Jenny
for throwing water on the couch.

October 6, 1709
I rose at 6 o'clock and said my prayers
and ate milk for breakfast.
Then I proceeded to Williamsburg,
where I found all well.
I went to the capitol
where I sent for the wench to clean
my room and when I came I kissed her
and felt her, for which God forgive me. . . .
About 10 o'clock I went to my lodgings.

I had good health but wicked thoughts,
God forgive me.

December 1, 1709
Eugene was whipped again
for pissing in bed and Jenny
for concealing it.

December 3, 1709
Eugene pissed abed again
for which I made him
drink a pint of piss.

BYRDS

JAMES BYRD JR.

June 7, 1998
This is the only day
for which I will be re-membered.

No one will recall what I ate
or if I read the newspaper,
but they will imagine
what I prayed for, to which God
I howled sanctuary in the night.

In all the 49 springs of my living
I did not betray the kindness
of strangers, even those who
wore the skin of my forbearers'
brutal masters. God forgive me.

Maybe I hoped after they beat me
and doused me with a pint of piss
that it would end there.
The blade's ragged teeth said otherwise.
I named it Jasper, the ugly ghost,
the white sheet with eye holes
to peer out at a shadow of myself.

They strung me to their pickup in the image
of the hanged man, ankles tied to the ankh
hitch like a ritual sacrifice. As they dragged me
down the dust road, I became Osiris,
seven pieces of immortality:
The teeth flung from mouth.
Each leg which could not run.
Hands which would never work again.
Arms unable to cradle my children safe.
Proud chest troubling the cemetery gates.
Skull with my brain still whole.

When I slipped away, I was glad to part ways
with memory, to only have to live this dying
once.

A wicked thought.
God forgive me.

BUCK HISTORY

Riding the subway in New York makes me daydream about commuting with a young Rosa Parks. In these fantasies, we are both fresh out of high school. We rock solid ponytails like erupting volcanoes and ice grill all the modern Bull Connors in their uniforms standing cross-armed the whole trip from Nostrand to 125th.

Instead of sitting at the front, we stretch our legs across six seats during rush hour, clapping hands and singing *Miss Mary Mack Mack Mack All dressed in BLACK BLACK BLACK* while businesspeople stand in the aisle. They ask us to move like they've been on their feet all day. We don't. We laugh when the train jerks them off kilter. There is no iconic photograph, but someone takes video with their phone and puts it on WorldStarHipHop.

I first had this daydream when a white man sat on my lap instead of the seat beside me. I waited for an apology, and got none, only shock as he began to whistle a happy tune. The livest fantasy came one day on a full-up downtown train. Back pressed to the doors, I shuddered as a man stepped in directly behind me, crotch nearly between my shoulder blades. I turned around to let him know he had to move. Side stepping next to me, elbows akimbo and in my face, he stared into his phone so I looked to see what required such an oblivious and clearly significant stance and this motherfucker was watching *Friends*.

My mind reeled to Rosa and I flanking him, pulling his earbuds out so he could hear us play the dozens on his life.

> *SPOILER ALERT: They stay white as hell!*
> *You in grad school? You writing a paper on misuses of hair gel?*
> *Hey, it's the 90s: time for you to have a fucking seat.*
> *Not literally, jackass, just stop colonizing my space.*
> *When they talk about this in school during February,*
> *nobody will speak your name.*

ANTIGONE'S LAST WORDS

I can only bury my flesh and blood
so many times before the king drives
my heaving corpse under a heap
of me-colored earth.

My brothers are no slaves, nor I.

I will master my own rope
sooner than submit to the graceless
shovel of man's spiteful laws.

ATTICA SERENADE

George Jackson: post-war slave narrative.
Nat Turner, 1971.
Maybe he died in the sun
and not the gas chamber
the way they wanted,

smiling and ready to meet the bullet.

We posted up two weeks before
we resurrected the man, Jackson
in the form of hostages and demands.

When they say the master's tools cannot
dismantle the master's house,
they don't tell you how to act when
the only tools are in
the master's weapon locker.
You have to make do.

No hands are idler than a prison guard's
before hell breaks out.
D yard became a guerrilla camp.
We called comrades on the outside
to bear witness.

Takeover or rebellion, never riot—
the governor's spit-shiny loafers.
A pig unfit for the sty
treating amnesty like he laid brick
in the walls of Jericho himself,
like no Pharaoh's army ever drowned.

Even the devil quotes scripture
when dawn arrives cloudy with teargas
and gunsmoke. Bullets like hailstones.
When the sun feels like a bad joke
nobody remembers the punchline to,

there are no sinners left but those
who blame the trees.
Bury all the evidence,
say we put that lead
in our own hearts.

Skkkrmble 4 Africa

Teacher says the Europeans got together and carved up the continent
like a Thanksgiving turkey in Berlin and I say that's really messed
up and aint nobody move or breathe too loud, just gets quiet as
a panther stalking its own shadow. Makes me feel like the wind
kicking up some old dust on a planet that used to have water.

AGENCY OF ORANGE

It might be an urban myth: that Van Gogh used orange to represent madness.

We read mythology into the flecks of fire in his beard. Into the gnarled crowns of demon goddesses he called sunflowers, the undulating landscape contrasted with crows, the dark night we read the stillness opposite the fury of a wild mind. Most people would call Van Gogh a redhead, but so often his reds collided with canary, filling the underbelly of cornfields. Can our orange speak the language of his? How do we know we see the same colors? When the kids in that commercial pass up the purple stuff for Sunny Delight, are their eyes wide with the same mania?

Orange is the color of the second chakra, the warm hearth of sex and gestation. Shade of a thousand ripe citrus burst open, drenching thirsty soil. Grove zest wafting behind a funeral of fruits, their skin peeled back in a soft cloud of Agent Orange.

Do we see in the same spectrum as the Vietnamese general looking at a black and white photo of himself before the solar flare of the Cold War turned his pigment to rust? When he glimpses the Kansas monochrome of his past, what right do we have to sympathize with his hellish Oz? Do we even share the same past? Do the Technicolor irises of our televisions blink in unison on Veterans Day? Can their circuitry recall naked children screaming napalm down an open road?

Agent Orange was an accident *or* another miracle of science. Its inventor was developing a way to adapt soybeans to a shorter growing season. Instead, his glorified alchemy concocted a potent herbicide. The U.S. military used 13 times the recommended amount to ensure that guerrillas could not hide. Women miscarried double-headed fetuses. Monsanto wrenched a million double helixes, U.S. vets and Viet Cong alike. This is a shade of American orange lit like the ends of cigars searing flesh.

Another urban myth is that most GIs returned from Vietnam to *Baby Killer!* spit at them. We can thank Rambo for that. Vietnam ended because the millions of people watching live combat on the nightly news raged against it while soldiers started fragging their commanding officers.

Somewhere in the middle of summer you forget what the fall looks like, and the decaying sidewalk foliage slips away in amnesia.

Our government has been killing civilians in the Middle East for nearly half of my young life. When I was 16, I was summoned to the principal's office, and, to my surprise, it wasn't for skipping Chemistry to make out with a boy other than the one I was dating. They assumed that I was leading a walkout scheduled for that week. I knew "Books not Bombs" was the slogan, but I wasn't leading any charges. I didn't believe teenagers in Hyannis could halt the shrapnel of Fallujah. I didn't yet know the lack of protest would beget an immortal war.

After listening to Principal Graves go on in a manicured drone about the nobility of youth rebellion and the necessity of repercussions, I told her that even though I didn't think walking out of school would produce immediate results, students had a right and a duty to take a stand. They weren't going to stop it by giving everyone detention anyhow.

That was over ten years ago. This morning I woke up from a dream where everyone I knew marched on Washington and hurled rotten jack-o-lanterns at the Pentagon until the newsmedia called us agricultural terrorists.

How long will we remain at Code Orange? We become accessories to occupation when we are angry but decide there is nothing that can be done. How many more decades will we live on high alert, whispering hideous secrets about the TSA? How can we see Van Gogh as a madman when his vases only bloomed with his own sorrow?

The streets may seem orange-barrel blockaded but let us not forget that they are *ours*. No one has ever won freedom by voting it into office, or paying taxes for weapons of mass destruction.

Alone, we will end up wearing convict orange to the funeral of our future. If we gather together like harvest fruits, we might also turn Agent Orange into saffron, the color of a monk's robe the moment before it is ablaze in the name of peace.

TOPSY (DIRECT)

Alls my life I had to fight or alls my life they welted me red and told me this was the only way I
would learn how to be decent but I don't know what use I have for all that when they kidnapped
me to parade around like snake oil on a tinker's cart for sale for use or display

I want to sleep

all day or crush my way out of this sideshow   eyes wicked enough to convince the devil
I was never born no how never had a mother just spectators and this pitchfork dug into my
thighs   it don't make sense Sears and Roebuck made dolls named for me   I's the
wickedest creature ever was   I reckon ain't no baby doll   Eva faith healed me for a sprint
but I come here already dead

reckoning that someday I'd be a gift for girls like Eva passed down like a hope chest to her
mulatto grandchildren a whole army of teeth a stampede of me collecting dust missing braids
pulling history in a rocketship made of bones

pull me back into the reef-plagued ocean that all wicked girls erupted from at the dawn of
time stolen and stealing and unwilling to be tamed by any current or camera or Ringmas'r
playing at being a god

PRESENT. (TENSE)

Every Finger is My Middle Finger

Blackface.
Police.
Oil spills.
Drones.
Rape culture.
Congress.
Wall Street.
Nuclear warheads.
Genocide.
Ableism.
The NSA.
Monsanto.
Facebook.
Straight people.
The President.
Historical amnesia.
One-sided class war.
Brownface.
Gentrification.
Climate change.
Student loans.
Evictions.
Displacement.
Alienation.
Hedge fund managers.
Golf.
Cosmetic surgery.
Fat shaming.
High-fructose corn syrup.
Prisons.
Neo-Nazis.
The IMF.
Bigots.
Clowns.
Fools.
Muhfuckers.
Assholes.

There are some masks we can never remove.
My hands are up, waving,
as the sea chokes, as the earth gurgles,
to protect myself from the unseen
eyes of predators everywhere I turn.
It's an old joke with no punchline,
guilty verdict with no conviction.
We've never stopped living in fear of
total annihilation at human hands
when these people are so capable of more
than we can ever pretend to *know*.
We've allowed the combine to churn
for far too long. It is consuming us now,
making us its fallow bride, laughing
at our feeble attempts to believe
that the future is winnable
for those at the bottom, scraping by.
Masks of skin hide pain, masks of paint
cover over what was there first, can
melt into air. Cities flood. Hope
burdens a generation with dreams
of what could have been stable lives
once. We could have belonged to land
instead of believing it belonged to us.
We have let slide decency to allow
for more living room, to carry on as if
everything was normal to begin with,
as if the past is a trophy wife, thin, pretty
and sweet as toothrot. They sell poison to we
peasants as if we cannot read, still.
They think we do not expect them.
And we will pay for it, inevitably, until
one of us collapses to the cold ground
which will never forgive us for its ruin.
My hands are up, waving,
and every finger is my middle finger.
Spare the blindfold if you plan to shoot.

My white family.   I will lend you my eyes, what they see,
My black family.   a pound of flesh makes a mote of difference
Babies crying.   to a hungry bullet.
Dogs barking.   Don't hide. Bear witness to this fearless
Rain.   disappearing act, evaporation, & return
Rain.   kissing the dust, the dirt, the mounds of
Rain.   bone with my wet, bloody mouth. I do not
Wind.   surrender. I take flight.

Aiyana Stanley-Jones Reported as "Disposition: Criminal"

Her barrettes must have
looked like razor blades
in the pre-dawn shadows.
Or maybe the gaps left

by lost baby teeth could
have smuggled narcotics
into show and tell. Or
maybe she muttered

you simple motherfuckers in her sleep
and that was enough
to qualify somebody's dead
babygirl for thug status.

Caution

If our legal system operates at the axis of ethics and logic, from which intersection of America was this bullet fired? Somewhere in the catacombs of precedence it is stated that if a strike incurs casualties beyond the intended target they are to be listed as enemy combatants, on principle. But who aids and abets the trigger-happy? Who blindfolds the executioner? Who beholds a child's corpse and lists her loss of life as the fine print of her neighbor's arrest warrant? Probably the same simple motherfucker who put her birth certificate on her daddy's rap sheet.

IF THE TABLES WERE TURNED

What would happen if we stopped and frisked the NYPD,
patrolled every precinct, groped their inner thighs,
confiscated weapons
         [we would find more than they ever have]
and drugs and money
         [which they have pinched for themselves].
We would repossess their flashy cars
to use for undercover missions
and if they tried to film us in the act
twist their arms, dislocate shoulders,
arrest them too, holler,
Deny Protect Deny!

What if they stood trial in an alley
or under a bridge—someplace quiet,
dark, and unofficial. They would be tried
by a "jury of their peers"
made up of mostly black people,
two men, ten women, Spanish-speaking,
majority Muslim, fair and objective.
Their guilt would be determined faster
than a dollar menu feast.

Even if we had beaten the confessions
out of them, and maybe 28 years later
when their children have grown
and their parents deceased,
someone will realize what we've done
and set them free. But we won't ever
serve time for that, or for opening fire
in the subway when we have them handcuffed,
or for opening fire after we've followed them home
and they are trying to empty dimebags
into their toilets, or for opening fire
as they go home at night,
or go home at dusk,
or leave home at dawn,
or when we open fire because they
ever call anywhere home to begin with.

What if OGs patrolled the suburbs
looking for Speedo-clad judges to assault,
or fracking lobbyists to take on rough rides,
or moving violations to turn into white-collar busts,
and no one batted a headline
over the handcuffed "suicides"
of Super PAC consultants.

No one would call us heroes.
They'd call it a riot
          epidemic
          slave revolt
          criminal
          petty
          demonic
          irrational
          savage
          barbaric
          primitive
          un-American

They'd spin it,
dig for thug selfies,
say we were no angels
then diagnose us
with Drapetomania.

Then they'd call us terrorists,
that's what.

The Process of Unveiling

A forest covers 13% of America,
home to all of its natural resources and art.

Every day the axemen come
       to carry the bodies away for kindling
           and axe handles,
leaving the willows sobbing and petrified.

At the edge of the forest
       stands a white marble statue
missing a nose, neck decayed,
       ass fallen entirely off.

Lifelike, gargoylian, a Bernini reject
       chiseled from unremarkable alabaster—
a metaphor for some old culturethief,
mute but always just having spoken, of course.

This bitch and her heinous microbraids.
This ocean of indulgent think pieces,
intellectualizing, widening the aperture
for whiteness, the way it is both background
       and subject while no one has unbent the back
of the half-naked teenager, or
       necromanced the loving parishoners.

This year has been a single question: did you hear about the—
       which one?

The news asks: isn't she one of the good ones?
       as if we will forget our Nana's shotguns
       and our ability to wring drinking water from gravestones.

I hate the distraction of her, and it has less to do
with proving the prowess of my own blackness than it does with
       the *illness* of lone white wolves,
       nuanced blackface in the avant-garde,
       the one before her, and the next,
       a million isolated incidents.

I'm exhausted from being crazy
            and dead and invisible
while the world's most boring performance artists
                flick matches at the tree line and call it rain.

THE CASTE LAND
for TSE

The people made a kingdom out of nothing. They were the people that didn't
make it across the water. They sat down right there. They say, "Let's make a
kingdom. Let's make a city of bones." The people got a burning tongue, Mr.
Citizen. Their mouths are on fire with song. That water can't put it out. That song
is powerful. It rise up and come across the water. Ten thousand tongues and ten
thousand chariots coming across the water.

August Wilson
Gem of the Ocean

I. THE OPENING OF THE MOUTH

February is the cruelest month, bleeding
Onyx onto the dead grass, binding
Grief to anger, firing
Hailstones to the unmoved pavement,
History filled our calendar, hoping
Flesh could un-dirge its voice, praying
A little life would matter.
Summer surprised us, brawling over the panhandle
With torrents of heat, we had a barbeque,
Pitched a tent for rain that ceased to come,
Cracked the lacquered shells of crab
Who had linked together fore the water took them.
¿Se puede vivir cada día como si fuera el primero?
When we were coming up, climbing the cement turtle,
My cousin and I knew to hide our eyes from men
Of fury, for fear and for protection we knew not.
Kristi, straighten your spine. We went
Into the grid of corner stores and churches,
Bought barrel juice, candy, returned alive.
I pace much of the night, stay north in the winter.

The swaying poplar gives no shelter,
And the sun bakes the earth
Every day, dries the revival well, pinches
Salt from unswept corners, there are
Only shadows cast from mounds of ancient bone
And brick. (Avoid shadows and furtive movements.)
I will show you the footage
Every shadow a creepy ass cracka
I will show you fear in a handful of gunpowder.
Love is lak de sea.
It's uh movin' thing,
But still and all, it takes its shape
From de shore it meets
You bring me armfuls of hibiscus from Port-au-Prince
And they sing of me, the earthquake boy, the hurricane
—Yet when we rose up from Drexciya
And shook the salt from our scars, you could not
See anything but gold teeth and mug shots.

We are a purgatory of resistance, unfuckwitable,
Looking into the sun and knowing its true name.
De mule uh de world

Mama Rêve, the old witch with no plumbing,
Knew all the future's business, foretold more
Of this city than the mayor himself.
With her cleaved deck of cards, she said
Here is you, child—the Drowned Prince of Songhai
(Behold his brazen leap from his captives!)
Here is Queen Sheba on a Lake of Glass,
The Man with Disks for Eyes, The Sistren of Cups,
Vessels stacked to the heavens, spilling libations like rain.
The Pimp With Three Canes, The Spinning Rim,
An unmarked card with only a pine box
Whose contents I cannot divine,
I do not find the Fool, Fear of Death by Liars.
I see stoops of people huddled over radios.
Thank you, If you see Ms. Laveau
Tell her I'll bring the gospel myself:
One can never quite trust preachers these days.

Unreal Country,
Under the black haze of a winter morning,
A congregation floated above the Mississippi.
I never knew how death unfurled so many,
Packets of Malaysian wavy, crisply-ironed silk,
Moans unending as were the forced silences, clap
On the two and four with the brass band of the reaper.
Barreling down Bourbon Street to where the Black Madonna
Kept the rhythm with a dry gourd on the stroke of noon.
There I saw the homie and hollered,
"You seen 'em blow the levee!
Those bones you buried in Aunt Jez' garden,
Have they brought you yams? Will it grow in summer?
Or have the dogs been at it again?
Blood! Muhfucka! Mirror! Cuz!"

II. A GAME OF SPADES

Draped in her bespoke alligator skin chair
Bejeweled with sapphire, refracting light on
The marble floor. A laser-cut diamond chalice
Perched between her cocoa butter fingers,
Caviar-infused lipstick on the rim of a Hennesey pool.
A golden-chained Anubis from the mantle weighed
The hearts of boychildren against the feather of Nuit
As her chinchilla draped, unruffled. And the air,
Thick with La Dalia Noir, devoured the room.

She'll be the first to smooth a wrinkle in her Sunday crown,
Light a Cuban at the bank drive-thru window,
Her hair silk wrapped around itself, smooth enough to speak
Proper English. Her mouth a moonlit enclave outlined
In red, bearing the mark of all that resists plague.
Her teeth polished pearl rosary beads she counts
With her tongue, repeating three times as good
Into the dark mirror pecking her tongue to incisor.

She waits, sipping slow at dinner, anticipating.
The scent of her velvet neck could be enough
To steer his ship towards her lace, her satin.
"Trifling, with a hard g, I remember the days
When they would doff their hats in winter
Just from the heat of my passing by."
A napkin wrung and tossed
Same as the phone, patience
Begins as a bop count, shrill cymbal:
Did something happen to him?
What the Wind say?
Counts her sturdy teeth, pops
A Xan down her throat, drifts.
Oh foul thief, where have you stowed my fire?
Even the wind barely speaks.
"What do you know? You don't even remember.
You don't know shit, and you ain't shit.
A blustered ruffle of the tablecloth.
Forgive my cursing, I'm on the edge of blue.
Down low. Worse than shook."

I would rather, I would rather go blind boy,
	Than to see you walk away from me, chile.
What shall we do tomorrow?
Chessboxin' and spades.
	I hope it rains, wash this out.
Close the sunroof to preserve the hair,
Unblinking gaze fixed on the silent door.

Before Cici's bd got out,
I took her up to see my sis Isis.
Early parole. She worried he'd find out
AIN'T NOBODY GOT TIME
Let her borrow my good shoes too,
Blue Loubitin pumps. I asked her
What she done with the bread from D
That he gave her for school clothes
And her stay-empty fridge. She smiled
Open, her 14k overlay fangs, shining,
And I nearly slapped her myself,
Won't say a word about it anyways.
Cuz ain't it a bitch, how we the ones stay
On trial even when they call us as witnesses.
New tennis shoes you can hide, but that?
And the double-slow light-up rims
On junior's beige sedan, out of place,
A Fauxlex for the baby.
AIN'T NOBODY GOT TIME
Four. The second youngest she said came wrong
Wrong time, wrong dick, wrong sign
And she had prayed on it, asked forgiveness
From the gap between her front teeth
On the way to the clinic. Got most of the way
And happened upon a statue of St Nicholas
Weeping, she swear fore Gawd, yessir.
AIN'T NOBODY GOT TIME
She say some nights she fix him a plate
Just forgetting.
And she let it get cold, she snuck out.
AIN'T NOBODY GOT TIME
AIN'T NOBODY GOT TIME
Peace Cici. Peace D. Peace Earth.

Peace God. The time, the place, the torture
This heavy act with heavy heart relate,
To die upon a kiss.

III. THE FIRE NEXT TIME

The river's wall is broken: a bouquet of teeth
Clutch and plunge into the wet depth. The sky
Huddles over brown-skinned earth, concrete,
Dem girls have gone. Ol' Man River must know
Something, don't say nothing. And the tow
Carries Blue Magic, cigarette cartons, slippers,
Red silk headwraps and women still in curlers—
All traces of upswept and unevacuated.
Dem boys gone too.
And their kin, the children of King's marches:
Gone, to void of rain, to last seen wearing.
There's an ol' man called the Mississippi
That's the old man I'd like to be
What does he care if the world's got troubles?
What does he care if the land ain't free?
But from behind, a cold blast, could've been a rapist,
The creaking bones, predator smirks at prey.

When the large rats zip past, bodies are near,
Dragged and sloppy, in the dry places.
Thinking about the gangster, my brothers' necks
And on the gangster my father's crown before them.
Black bodies naked, bloated on the low mud
Bones askew or unfolding like the wings
Of Addie Mae, Carole, Cynthia & Denise.
Unreal country which never lets us be children,
Only thick, cool. Juicy and digestible.

The rats will stir up what men don't find,
So the march, trumpet bleats in time,
Pinky, oiled, spread and clapping
In the California day heat, tapping
Dat ass on dat ass, pouring champagne
On dat pussy for the camera, four smiling lips.
And the culluhed girls sing

Do da doot da doot da doot doot doot da doot
Oh Oh Oh Ohoh oh oooh oh oh
Oh foul thief

Zimmerman.
Wafer.
Officer.

Too real City
Like a brown fog in February.
Mr. Bokini, the Lagos hustler,
Long haired, with fists full of cocoa
O-dee O Zees: paper, on sight
Asked me in mash Creole
To lunch at the Mercer
& a weekend with his crew in Biscayne.

At the violent hour, when feet and ass
Leap up from concrete, when the cyborg calculates
As in the sprinting web deep calculating,
Blind Willie Lemon deepens his shovel at the crossroads.
At the violent hour, the night that yearns
To return home and carries the refugee back to war torn.
The admin, home by sundown, fills the dish rack,
Primes her pilot light, sets to baking.
Out her window, starlight is a dying ember of the past,
And what burns brightest fades faster.
She prays over every bite.
I Blind Lemon, with muscled fingers
Peeped too, and knew what came next,
And waited too for the black republican,
The young money, arrogant fitted cap cocked
To an authentic angle. He speaks of Carson
Until she grows weary, and she is quick to tire
Even as he intrudes upon her blouse,
Tolerated only as a gesture to his wallet
And framed diplomas, and I Lemon
Saw the turn of the sheets, agonizing
At a room without fire, I who have waited
For Eshu in that dark and muddied moonlight
And walked with the Pauper's field piled dead.
He allows one kiss. Goodbye. As a gesture,
Cops his way out the door in the darkened hall.

The window becomes a mirror, only aware of her.
And she barely recalling the hands, the lips,
Glad to be alone, to wrap her hair in red silk,
Clicking the playlist, "Bitch Betta Have My..." as
She stomps upon the familiar floor.

"Allaying both their fury and my passion,"
All throughout a nation, up Pennsylvania Ave
O country country, the mournful wail that creeps
Off into the fog in the low weight of the Mississippi.
The high pluck of a banjo forgetting its gourd-self
And the clapping time in some sweatsugar juke
Where laborers set up at noon, where the door
Of Oral Roberts swings
Wild, feathered, syncretism of snake-green illumination.

The river still sweats
Oil and tar
The barge left
By the low levee,
                    (Or does it explode?)
Rushing wake
Wide
Starboard, spar with masthead
The people watch
Dogs drifting
Down Nawlins reach
Past Sawdust Bend
O Solomon don't leave me here
Cotton balls to choke me

Hov and Bey
Beating oars
An oaken hull
Dipped in gold
Blood and green
The swole water
Coasting abrupt
Category Five
Raging the catwalk
Flow downstream.

The organ sings
White powers
Solomon done fly
Solomon done gone

"Jack Johnson want to get on board
Captain he says 'I ain't haulin no coal!'
Fare thee, Titanic, fare thee well!"

"Then must you speak
    Of one that loved not wisely but too well,
    Of one not easily jealous but, being wrought,
    Perplexed in the extreme; of one whose hand,
    threw a pearl away richer than all his tribe;"
I said nothing. How could I blame the man?
"In Brooklyn row houses
Me and the Rza connect
Empty with gravity
Cracked skin and grit
My people expect,
Who humble,
Who nothing—ha."

To Havre de Grace I came

Blazing blazing blazing blazing
I prayed with my legs, shout me out
My legs shout me out

Blazing

IV. DEATH BY FIRE

Fred Hampton, the Chiraq kid, half-century dead,
Forgot the rolling traffic, the concrete flat lurch
And the power and people.
A tide below our cities
Picked his bones clean, quiet.
As he fell and fell he passed
Over only his youth's urgency.
My people
Who ghostride the wind,
Consider Fred, who was once bold and black as you.

V. HOW LIGHTNING SAY

After the medic blanket on their faces
After the deafening quiet on the grass
After the struggle in every stone corner
The courthouses and the corner stores
Prison and Palace as echo chamber
Of lightspeed summer somewhere green
All the way live, got dead
We who were live, on the way
With some time.

Everyone thirsty, only got rock
Rock and thirst and sidewalk
The air above, a wide street around skyscrape
Are we thirsty enough for this
Would we forget the drinking gourd for this
Fume of breath and scorched earth
If the water were clean
City jaw wired tight, toothless
Here no man survives, unscathed, clean
No woman granted peace, solace
By the heat lightning, the tumult,
No escape cross the bridge, even going home
But bloodied, covered faces gnash dreams
From block to block
If there weren't thirst, clean water

And not rock
If there was rock
And no thirst
And thirst
A dream
Oasis from rock
If there were only rest
Not the sirens
And glass breaking
But sound of dreaming
The way the starlings murmur
Wishhh wishhhhh wishhhhh wish
But there are no dreams.

Who that you carry with you?
And what is a river anyway?
I looked, you, me and some haint
Down the block some, like an Amen
Ricocheted
Cuz some bullet missed or never flew,
Golden child still swaggin in a hoodie
You need not begrudge in public.
You blessed and highly-favored child
—But who that creeping at your side?

Why the church bells still holler out
When the mothers stone face the camera
Who are those hooded hordes swarming
Over endless brick, tripping across potholes
Circled by solar grace
What city will rise
Crumble and shift and burst into the white noise
Blown up project towers
Chicago Baltimore Detroit
New Orleans St Lou
Unreal

A woman picks her natural out
And a choir sings out in that trill
And the child-sized rats through the alleys
Shrieking and gliding with dirty claws
And burning crosses turnt upside-down in air
Phone wires become ancient shoelaces
And all that has drowned cannot be quenched.

In this rot this sprawl among progress
In the light-polluted lavender sky, every tree beckons
Above the trains and graves, around the scrapers
There the decimated towers, a well for tourists.
Windowless prison, the closed gate
Decaying meat in the hot dayglare trash

A pigeon on a rooftop
Whowho whoooowhowho
Scattered by a thunderclap, Oya's breath
Bringing change.

Hudson sunk low with bodies of dead trees
Waiting for change, while the vast slate sky
Lowers to spiral, over Chrysler
The ghetto stalking the sky silently
Then lightning opened its vibrato mouth
BUCK
Ain: what is left to give?
Love's a riot in my tired bones
The quicksand giving in to the past
Which no broom can sweep
There but for the grace of God go we
Which they leave out at funerals
Or whisper delicately among wisteria
Or tuck in with the eviction notice envelopes
Left where we no longer stay
BUCK
Ain Soph: I know the hour comes
But once. We dream of the inherited earth
When cell blocks open, each a prisoner
Thinking of open blocks, confirms in each a prison
Only in the dark, where ghosts whisper
And bring forth Harriet Tubman
BUCK
Ain Soph Aur: the fields call and respond
Joyfully, to the hand that sowed
The air was still, your blood would call, respond
Joyfully, when called, juba
In time to freedom.

I sat in the sand, with the tide rising
Eating jellied eels with distant thought
Can land be returned, or lineage?
And the rockets' red glare, the bombs bursting in air
But when do we fly like Solomon? Oh Sugar Man
The crown'd king of Babylon, tumbling.
These crumbs set upon my ruin
Why I wish you would,
Headeye's hollerin one mo 'gain
Ain. Ain Soph. Ain Soph Aur.

It's a new dawn.   *It's a new day.*   *It's a new life.*

National Surveillance Agency

We've triangulated your favorite positions
so your best bet is the shovel,
to dig a new tunnel. Try evolving
to use echolocation. Hold your
meetings in the dead sea.
Pray for a power outage.
Leave your phone on the altar
of any saint but Anthony
because we are doing our best
cartography on your nervous systems.

We have plans to lay fiber optic cables
in the foothills of Bedouin strongholds.
Watch for smoke through an infinite lens.

This is for your protection,
the homeland, and Jesus
who wept salt for your sins.
If you move to upend the tables
of bankers in our temple,
you will nail your own pine box.

This is the resurrection
of J. Edgar's wettest dreams,
undead, loosed, cyborg,
preparing for the inevitable
possibility   (decay?)
Our eyes wide, calculating
                        waiting.

MODERN DAY MEDUSA
for Rekia Boyd

Perseus shot blind,
catching her reflection
in the rearview, never
looking her in the eye,
already stupid as rocks,
shielded by his badge.

He feared the gold giants springing
forth from her, and the Pegasus
born a pallbearer gorgeous and
terrible as his mother.

The Argonauts sent her family
a bag of snakes as a warning
against protesting
the hero's crimes.

The prosecutor Athena
sewed serpents in the lapel
of her favorite power suit.

Euripides the stenographer
noted the chorus of tragedy masks
lamenting a hubris
so reckless its breadth
cannot be named.

ILLEGAL

205,000 salted wounds.
Parents taken from children.
Surviving boats shoved back
across Mediterranean divide.
Apartheid flooding Gaza.
Detention without charge.
Force fed without trial.
Bullets across the US border.
Mass graves in Texas.
A mother's carrion becomes
a valley of dry bone.

Fallible humans make
fallible laws make
plums bust open
and pits sucked dry.
Torture. This world
begs the question:

if a neighbor arrived
in the darkest part
of night bloody
and calling your name,
would you answer,
or fire shots
through your own
front door?

CHRISTOPHER STREET

How many times will they pull Marsha P. Johnson from the river?
Every year, too many white candles for brown girls.

Some days I worry my friends won't make it home.
Some nights I consider spiking a paint key
into the eyes of bigots.

Once, at Thanksgiving, my brother looked at me,
laughed, and said "Dyke."
I punched him in the mouth then ate dinner.

More than once, I have been called
a faggot out of passing car windows
and kept walking.

I lost track of every cunt men
have called me
when I ignored their mouths.

We all look over our shoulders alone,
but if my body turned up
they might look for the killer,
and if my body turned up,
it might make the evening news,
and if my body turned up,
they would call me by my right name,
and if our bodies showed up
the way they did for wedding cake,
and if *Vanity Fair* showed up
for Cece like it did for Caitlyn,
no president could tell Jenicet
to shut up and eat his free shit.

This poem is a list of names.
This poem isn't mine to write,
but who am I to point to the pauper's field
and be quiet about my missing sisters' bones?

VEGETABLES WHEN CAKE IS NOT ENOUGH

Burning down the cane fields
is a kind of damage control

as is plucking out a rotten tooth.
The wind will take care of the apples

overripe, brown and heavy, swinging.
God will not blow you away even if you beg.

No one is irredeemable, but ground must break,
soil be tilled, and the table full with harvest

before a predator can claim growth has occurred.
If you feel doubt, a raggedy *both-sides* lodged

in your throat, remember this.
Not everyone has the luxury of choosing

whom to believe when they didn't hear you say
NO. Our options are always limited at first—

skittish trips outside only when necessary,
when the supermarket swirls, focus on one color.

For me, green. No one has no one to hold us back
from ending our own breath while marked damaged,

but feelings are facts. Brethren may choose to play
the devil or his advocate if or when you open your mouth.

Sistren may call you a liar in the daylight
and weep alone knowing it could be them

when the moon uncages them. Family
is not a blood oath, cannot bind you.

Do not forget this when they come for you
with flame and pitchforks. Never flinch.

UNLUCKY BUILDING[1] FOR CHARLESTON EMANUEL AME CHURCH

.day that on all, you hide can't I, out cried rock the And
(But there's one thing you can count on, that's death. Death hates God.)[2]
What is left both black and sacred? I run to the rock.
?name His out called children his when God was Where. missed He.
with a halo of bullets, for my unholy black.
nigger me call to thought uncle my, nine was I When
he play-launched in the middle of the war we call home.
war the of proud, mast full at waving flag a is He
and bought him a Happy Meal for being a good boy.
vest fine a in pig the dressed cops, him found they when And
One, Two, Shoot, One, Two, Shoot, take us to the bridge BangBang!
,rhythm unchained its for named they song old an is This
And couldn't he have been my neo-Nazi uncle?
?worship of house father's my been have it couldn't And.

1 a form created by Sean DesVignes, read from the ground floor up the stairs.
2 Ornette Coleman, Interview with *Wax Poetics* 2007.

ON PROPER FLAG BURNING

First, cut out the field of stars
as if you are light pollution.
Hand pinking shears to a boy scout.
Instruct him to liberate white from blue
& prune around all five tips
of fifty.

Once he has unfettered the chattel galaxy,
stack the stars in a linear constellation
and feed the hollowed out blue into the licking fire.

If you are not quick it will catch
the breeze and be turned into
the press conference necktie—worn to spin
its mannequin in a more humanitarian light.

Cock your helmet to one side,
then give the candycane stripes
to the Hollywood bombshell
with Vegas-bright eyes and serpent smile.
Drape it over the airbrushed tones of her bare skin
tactfully while the awkward stepfathers
and the other lonely petitioners
tear thirteen off one by one in their minds.

When they are done fill a basket
with the blood-colored scraps and take them
to a woman who was an air raid siren
in the "Duck and Cover" days.
Have her stitch them together by hand
so you can lay them down as scarlet borders
on the maps of every city in this country.
They will burn on their own.

The white stripes can be shred
into the Morse code of highway lines
or razored neatly on glass coffee tables.

White as snowcapped,
as the first voters. Be sure to burn them
in cross formation, three pairs, and say:
Flags are about heritage, not hate or
I watched him die on YouTube or
Can't we all just go out to the bar with the President?

Orange ash will lift, so toss the stars
from a distance. Pretend they are
heavy as horseshoes.
See if the fire can catch them.
A flick of the wrist for forty-nine.
As each smolders to black
recite the names of your heroes
without your teeth chipping.

The last star is yours to swallow.
Gulp hard and look sober.
May it be the lights coming on.
May it begin a countdown to launch.

May the zero hour find you
knife clenched tight between teeth,
a flammable banquet of falsehoods
before you,

                    reflecting the early light.

FUTURE. (TENSE)

Aeon of Horus
(an invocation)

Age of Basquiat crown'd & conquering children.
Yung niggas run everything, even pyrite America.
We twerk sweat stains into cotton, libations
for headless kings all through the night.

The onyx sky is the first roof
we learned to fuck under.
Faded hours' lack of stars,
just where we stay, where we leave
and come back to, and fly.
Bless us, unfurling acres above.

The moon howls at us, sun.
We, the children of dead men
torn apart and re-member'd,
by our mothers' firm hands.
We, a plume of untamed
smoke in a bare-bulb room.
We the ricochet of stray bullet,
the shine of gold fangs.
We Buckbuck Bangbang.

No one stacks paper without
seeing the wig blown off the top
of pyramids and replaced
with a surely white eye.
Pay it. No mind.

Holler out instead:
We don't die, we multiply!
Never Lazarus, just the first light
glimpsed by the resurrected.

Our path: radiant
Our time: now.

MOCKINGBIRD

I don't know how to   make   words,
I've got traffic jams stuck in my teeth.
Call me Mockingbird.
        I've got so many songs to tell you.
My voice, it's only lightning humming,
just [electric current] just magnets just
I'm a dummy and the whole world's a ventriloquist,
but I'VE GOT A BIG MOUTH,
the fingers punch destinations,
spin of a needle, they send me signals
like half-finished love letters that rarely get to the point.

I just wish I could dance.

I rest my jaw in the dead nights truck driving.
I'll rise right before the sun.

They built me like a hand,
scattering so many seeds, so please,
don't speak about me like I'm too old to understand you.

Let me tell you a secret:
The alphabet has a sequel.
I know they haven't taught you about it
but the pauses   between   words
they're   just   as important.

Space is the possibility of electrons moving,
it's not nothing, it's not silence.
Your body is electric too, and so
nothing is ever perfectly still.

There is so much potential between all the noises
you cough up.
You put your teeth to the microphone grates,
and say "shake lightning
up out of your throat,"

and now glass poppies,
platinum sphinxes, snare//bass.
windchimes in windless places.

Your grammar echoes endlessly.
Every half-muttered bedroom promise
bounces in a cat's cradle of foreverwaves
across houses and forests.

Everybody knows all the towns
have the same disc jockey voice types,
but scan the horizon,
strain your eyes across the broadly-casted fields
of voices and you'll find me.

I'm the one who glum shucked
into your grandparents' houses
and told them about Pearl Harbor.
Every sound I make will never die,
so I'll ricochet through your dreams.
Everyone acts like a Victrola's outdated
but nobody asks when
you're going to run out of electricity.
The ck-chunk kick of a ghetto blaster
won't be outdone by downloading
so stop running around acting like
you don't need shoulders
to carry your music.

I'll be there when every soldier is sent rowing,
all bows pointed at heaven,
at the satellites,
at anything beyond our own dull drone
when myth ascends mouths,
when mouths become sky,
when your stories become constellations,

when you realize that all stories are one epic
and all the ears are one open place
where you can put your mouths.

I'll be there,
my name chiseled out of radius,
out of circles
and waves.
Call me Mockingbird,
but my name is the Wireless.
My father was a Tesla coil
and my mother was a lullaby.
Follow the sound of my voice
and keep the rhythm right (right?).

Just listen.
I've got so many songs to tell you.

SUN RA SPEAKS TO GUCCI MANE

Are

you guilty?

"Bitch, I might be."

They say   you said to

the white judge. But I say,

WHY MUST YOU LIMIT YOURSELF

TO JUST ONE   SMALL BLACKNESS?

to a planet you have carved   into the skin of

your face.

You are ob-sessed with the cold, with the solid state

of water. Brrrr the glint of your gold, but it ain't Horus, or even

the sand, it might be the record sk-k-kipping on the same dust speck

of what they call history.   My story is the mystery but that don't mean

that I forget.   When the judge looked me in the eye and said, "I don't think

I've ever seen a nigger like you before." I looked at him and said   **No,**

and you never will again. You see, my algorithm was born on Saturn with no mother

or father, like rhythm, the way Ornette say. I see the drum in the tree before the lightning *hit* it,

cuz my eyes wide open like the arms of Venus without Molly poppin, without slurring on a blunt

object aimed for the backa my head. Space don't have no trap spot 'cept black holes, or worm

holes tore   through the velour of dimensions. I don't believe in violence at. all. Cuz that's not

the way we do thangs in my orbit.   I wouldn't fight Hitler, nevermind   a soldier trying to

express an appreciation for the joyful noise that I make.   Now your equation look   a little bit

more finite. But that don't mean   you can't compose yourself into the cosmos' groove. That

don't mean that you need to be stuck on that old rusty gun clap of what you call a woman when

you think she can't hear, or don't care. But why buy old sounds when you could shoot into the

atmosphere radiant, anew, and get solar flare lit   up?

FLAMBUOYANT

(for Wolfie)

The man on the wire   between the two towers is
the queerest part of the skyline,   taunting police with his balancing,
            agile as the bat of false eyelashes.

His feet made of feathers,   his heart a granted wish,
                        his dance

a metaphor for the street acrobats below,
the ones who live on a tightrope
            between criminal and freak,
                        who are as graceful as swans in a street brawl.

The typical city grid winds out from a central muscle
                                    pumping concrete rivers,
                        from above, it might be hard to tell,
                but on the ground, every day you
            can catch us playing Huck Finn
and fighting the current.

This is the song of the bathroom barbershops with
clipped and lopsided specials, of the holes in
every layer of our clothing,

Of the risk taking librarians and petty hustlers,
the down low queens and diesel femmes,
the soldier rethinking the war in the street or the desert,
Of the activist slain for speaking, which is his currency.

We are a chorus of street artists evading trains and cops,
baristas who are into BDSM, teachers who hate textbooks,
butchers and cashiers, strippers and busdrivers,
paper shufflers and toilet cleaners,
window dressers by day, DJs by night,
dust on the wind, blood through the veins.

We spin the world faster than gravity,   and oooooo eeeeeee
                                    we got the moves!

Of course, there are days when the sun pierces our eyes
like light in a tear gas canister,
when nothing but nothing has gone right for our whole lives,
and we are untethered from the earth,
prey to our own hedonism or shame.

Those days, in these places where the people are so many
and the empathy so distant, we may find ourselves
death dropping in bathroom stalls,
putting tacks on math teachers' seats,
succumbing to our own inertia,
hands trembling when the nearest bartender hands us
a drink and a kind glance after a terrible phone call.

The weight that creeps onto our chests
as we try to sleep is the rock that Sisyphus pushes,
and yes, we are him too.

There is no shortage of madness in our balancing act,
and yet we find ways to soar,
even when the ex moves in down the block
with their new partner,
or when you can't claim your own identity at work
because they would fire you on the spot.

We who spin the earth manage to create cures
for the awful distance between the sky
and the streets, however minor, however unhealthy,
we're coping with all the hideous facets of hate and normality
long enough to keep fucking up the pristine lie of tranquility.

If aliens came to Earth and asked for one word to describe us
I would say *buoyant*.

We manage to dream even when strong currents snag our feet.
We go on to living another day,
daring the wicked world to take another shot.

Requiem for the Bees

When all the young are older,
our guarana-drugged taurine children
will seem a generation of the impractical to us,
not only because we will be set in our ways.
By then we will have seen the Model T
which once carried our encyclopedias
and snake oil chug through decades
shedding cranks and poorly-designed frames
until all of our information comes with
sun roof options, satellite radio,
four touch screens, and a camera on the bumper
warning of all that's behind us.

Green tendrils that once curled soil in the base
of their question marks are being usurped
by square compressed crop circles of metal
and silicone that most of us can't translate.

In the future, ratchet-jointed Caligulas will oversee the
synth-pollenated arboretums that you've abandoned,
and we will have to explain to an entire generation
what your droning sounded like without any reference point
that isn't a mechanical Zzzz snored in office buildings
or drooled onto the pillows of our ears
from the napping machines in our dens.

You will be figments that populate infants' dreams
and send them wailing across nights.
You will be boggarts and banshees.
Your necessary choreography: retold as
spook-dance fabrication by grandmothers.
Your hexagon hearths of lush amber:
weaved into lofty tales of evil fortresses
you erected in our attics to keep thine enemies close.

We are not nemeses, my beloveds.
Your flight patterns just map
a perpendicular line across our

Magnetzoic Era Progress Projection charts.
So you, small, frizzy beasties,
impede upon our conquest.
You have no place in our Coltan mines,
our fracked city grids, our porous ozone,
or our petroleum-based gardens.

No, you just don't fit into the plans because
you are efficient and carbon-based.
Your collaborative movements towards survival,
they are practical, archaic;
they look too much like a single organism or
a Marxist gathering.

Your operational evenhandedness of tasks
makes our employment system
look obsolete by comparison,
and the sheer elegance of your collective thought,
that is what we'll steal
from the reflections in your exoskeletons.
That's the lesson we'll scan into our blackboards
during extinction week in the elementary schools.

You won't be erased, no.
We will upload your gathered drowsy embraces
and your work songs,
and your pregnant royalty onto our mainframe.

The wind from your dead wings will start up
the operating system we all rely on
to get closer to becoming of one hive.

History from the Future

Hello ancestors,
I've come here to give you a book called *The Future*.
It's a quick read, even for you old abacus-eyed cave toads.
Page one:
space aliens
page two:
the internet
all the other pages are blank.
This is a warning for the empty pages being filled in
as we gather up our lung dust here.
You cowboys are living on the frontier lines.
2001 was the year the manifold bared its skull.
The year peeled back its follicle-dusted fields
and showed us the zeroes and ones that dreams are made of.
Humans became wiiPods of mirror, shuffle shuffle,
    shuffling reflections of themselves
        across the wires until their movements looked real enough.

You here: collected, listening, you might become cinema,
might become celluloid dissolving and
giving way to the white white screen of cloudy sky.
I didn't click back here to preach, though,
just wanted to tell you some things, for instance:
The Wikcyclopedias list Steve Jobs as Johnny Appleseed.
The future's schoolchildren will learn him like Eli Whitney...
everyone will know what he invented,
but nobody will remember why it's important.
The last almanac says that in 2005 many of you
erected baseball card shrines to yourselves,
amassed a small cult following,
and in 2073, strangers will leave digital frankincense and candle wax.
If you play your cards right shuffle shuffle
    the temples won't waterlog,
lay the foundation of your personality perfectly even.
If you cement mix your statistics, heroes, favorite movies,
your body type smoothly enough,
every last one of you will die sacred,
        so don't be shark jumpers, click.

Be scripture,
		be scripted, fake it. You are celebrity.
					It is already written. You are stars, so shine.

My almanac lists 2085 as the year your children
collect the good seasons of your youth,
trying to shuffle click catch you glamourpussed golden,
instasmooched with red-plastic-cup mouths,
catching attention in your gloves, the old pastimes.
You will be grandparents, milk-eyed inheritances,
funeral processions—part-tabloid, part-epitaph,
your favorite quote semi-permanent etched
"in loving memory" by those that slid their prints
across the touchscreen of your analog wrinkled skin.

In 2142, the almanac says the children learn you Wild West,
call you quickdraw, pioneers, call you desert treaders of mind,
call you pony expression, lightspeed postal service,
call you wall post, outpost, galloping with wireless muscles.
The children call you those of many faces,
quicksand forgotten,
but build you holy.

All of you will be archangeled in the shifting mausoleums.
You will rest in wirebox tomb, iMemorial, until 2486
when the sea gets amnesia
from swallowing the last blood Truemerican
and softens stone to erase your voice
from the annals of soundwave.

Why have I come back to find you?
Soon everyone will lose interest in rocking chairs.
The porches will corrode, but the bunkers will survive.

You are the architects of me,
and you're building history right now with your eyes.
The only for-sures of the future are space aliens and the internet,
I'm not tinting your path rosy-glass eyelided,
I'm just clicking back to tell you that this is the year
the borders break or rise thicker skinned than baseball gloves.

I am history book digital.
You will build walls.
You will break it off by changing status,
shifting citizen, shuffle love, clicking *it's complicated*.

This is what's written now,
but you're erasing it, maybe not here,
but you will edit every day, unknowing.
It's not worth alarming you to the heart attack war should bring
      at middle age,
or the story-perfect change of heart you *could* have, Ebeneezer eyes.
No, I'm just tonguing possibility in your cheeks.
I'm altering the book by telling you this,
I'm digging wormholes.
    So I will preach now, just one commandment: tangle fingers
        instead of power cords.
            Do you still have power cords?

Did they abandon the pianos yet to the graveyards?
I will not psalm book you rattlesnakers,
but if you tangle tangle in the shuffle storm
and love so the walls don't grow skins,
you will keep the hate militia and the religion of self
from weed walking through the garden so the statues can keep
      their limbs click.
Just tend. Just be tender. Don't be click.
    If you forget what's real, don't worry.
Reason was the first epidemic.
In my time, no one remembers that alchemy was the first antidote—
turning logic into fool's gold,
or that magic went the way of medical leeches.
You would do well to unreason.
The zero one zero zero grids are your chickenpox,
your gradeschool quests for objective truth.
Shuffle 010010110 around the neighborhood so you don't click
    shingles in 2073.
Don't bubonic in the Bluetooth centuries, scratch now.
    if you don't hologram me into forgetfulness,
you won't commit *your* children to the graveyards.
We are a wirebound humanhood umbilical,
and if you don't hi-fi like your parents and don't pat your back for trying,

you might click forsake the graveyards,
you might ascend digital, you might Lazarus.com, breathe.

I just came to give you this book and let you know
that the blank pages fill themselves
when your feet shuffle shuffle out to the street and lift.

WITCH HUNT

The heirs to the Great Land Heists
parcel and fence the shoreline.
Their blood: slick with thieving.
When they call your name and ask
you to answer for the heresy
of your being, disobey gravity.
Untether your shame & levitate
like caskets don't come in your size.
Fire is a straw man's fear, so
extinguish their torches, you river,
you cauldron. Open the sky
with the obsidian mirrors of your eyes.
Call on the golden marrow of
your ancestors. Burn your face
into their retinas so they recognize
the ghosts who uproot them, who
bloody their dreams. We
who return, remain.

REFUSE

Even in the poor places here we wear the blistered hands
of invisible children upon our feet, sprawling waste on every inch,
waiting for the callous-fingered shadows to pluck and toss
all we see as ill-fit to live indoors.

In the night, the wind in this city speaks of the
asbestos patches around school yards
and the legacy of burned buildings.
All the co-ops and green initiatives Gentrified, U.S.A.
aren't going to alter history or change the sound
of a torn plastic bag on grey snow.

It is said that America's number one pastime is shopping, probably
because throwing shit away is a chore to most people.
In France wine is paired with food from the same region.
They call it *terroir* or "sense of place." To know a land.

For about eight months I ate almost entirely from dumpsters
out of poverty. I can't say I got any sense of the land
because all of it tasted like disrespect for everything that grows.

One time a cop drove by us as we were elbow deep in trash bags
and said, *I'm not going to tell you to stop but that's gross.* He wasn't wrong.

With the sticky, orange glaze and onion flakes crusted under our nails,
it was hard not to wonder about too much, the bagels going stale, and all
we were trying to salvage that was not worth consuming in the first place:

smushed pastries and sugar scraps like us, looking for some place that hasn't
yet been claimed by the big-wallet men and their devil-chested wives,
some moon-crater part of America where the pox never danced
upon the brow of a native, where the guns slept in silence,
where everyone might be sustained, and even the bones used wisely.

Let me find that place,
on this earth,
in this country.
Somehow, let it be.

Unfinished Letters From the Most Popular Kid in the Psych Ward

To Arbour Psychiatric Hospital:

Had my brain waited six months to collapse, I would have read the news articles about the number of facilities in your network that had to be shut down, about the number of untrained staff you had, the lack of staff overall, about your record profits for a non-acute hospital, or about the sexual assaults. I never would have allowed them to bring me to you. Instead, I was left with a cousin who had also been trapped in one of your disgusting halls screaming at my biological father to get me out of you.

To my twelve white roommates who called 911 when I was in crisis without notifying me:

What if the cops had shown up first? Instead? What if they killed me? You didn't even think about that. It was always about your safety (from me) first. I can't imagine the torment it must have caused you when my mind stretched like elastic, when I could only talk in circles, when it never actually felt like I was fully asleep. Look, I know you tried. I threw a glass of juice at a wall, not at our roommate. You didn't know what else to do. I was angry because one of you wouldn't call the one person I trusted, who is also black. I was angry because my phone was bricked and I deactivated my Facebook account. I was angry because our roommate, the one I threw the glass past, she wouldn't explain why she wouldn't contact him, just said she wouldn't. I did not want to hurt her, or anyone. All of you were too busy trying to figure out what was best for me without ever actually asking me. I threw the glass past her. It was disturbing, and I am sorry, but that was frustration, not a threat. She was a foot away from me. I had been a shattered person for almost a week by that point. It was Easter, I remember.

To the all-black EMT squad that responded to the call:

I have never seen anything as magnificent as you, before or since. When you arrived, I was in my room calming myself down, alone. It was the first real clarity I had felt in a week, and then you showed up. I shook every one of your hands and introduced myself, and apologized that your time was being wasted. You told my roommates that if you removed me from the house it would be kidnapping, and maybe if I was more aware of what had been happening inside me, I would have asked for a psych eval. Thank you. You were water.

To the friend I trusted, who arrived the next day:

Thank you for doing something that I know was hard for you, for holding my hand, even though we had been fighting for months. Thank you for talking calmly to me, and telling me that you were concerned. I had never experienced anything like this, and it was terrifying. Thank you for making sure I had insurance before taking me to the hospital for an evaluation, and for sitting with me while it was conducted.

To the woman at the hospital who did the evaluation:

When I said I didn't think group therapy was going to help me in my current state, I meant it, and I don't know why you refused to listen.

To the staff of the outpatient facility:

No one explained what the group was for—why that assemblage of people were all in the same room. There was the white man who got red in the face yelling that he hated "recruiters" and the mother from Roxbury grieving her murdered son. It was too much, so I left the halfway through the first day. When I came back the second day, I brought my oldest friend, who flew across the country to be with me. You instructed me to stay in the waiting room. You took her somewhere. I don't know how much time passed. I went looking for her, and when I didn't find her, I sat back down. You called me into another room, and within five minutes, I was strapped to a gurney in the back of an ambulance being taken to a psych hospital that was a ten-minute walk away.

To J, my oldest friend:

Isn't it just like a woman of color to fly from California to show up my white "friends" who wouldn't walk three blocks?

To Arbour Psychiatric Hospital:

The lithium made me incapable of walking steady, made me hear roaring crowds outside the hospital, made me scream in bed. I put a golf pencil in a cupcake, and said something incoherent about a puzzle, so you sent me to your most intensive unit. A tiny, weasel-looking man said he didn't like the way I was looking at him. He called me nigga and slapped my hand. Nobody did shit about it and I was standing directly in front of the nurse's station. One of the nurses thought bringing her glasses down the bridge of her nose would convince us to do anything she told us to. The first time I refused the cup full of meds, she tried that trick and it didn't work. I demanded to know why there were so many pills, and was told "you know what they are." I knew I was prescribed lithium, that's one drug. Not Ativan, not Risperidal, not children's Benadryl. I knew you were drugging me to knock me out because I wouldn't stop walking up and down the hallway, because there was literally nothing else to do except maybe drool on the TV screen sometimes. I knew I had the right to refuse. I didn't know I would spend the better part of a month feeling trapped in the hospital because I was "oppositional." Given that during that time there were at least seven days that I slept on a flame-retardant mattress with no sheets, blanket, or pillow, I'm not sure how you charged me thousands of dollars it took me years to pay off.

To the hospital psychiatrist:

Why didn't you ask about trauma? You just played guessing games, flipping a coin between schizophrenia and bipolar and didn't listen when I told you about what the lithium was doing to me. Why did you wait two weeks to ask the question: you know why you're here, right? I said yes, but what you were asking seemed more specific than because I couldn't sleep, or even because when I listened to the radio at 3 am, I thought an infomercial sounded like my dead dad and dead uncle playing the dozens on the medical industry that allowed them to die before either one reached 50. That's why I told you I worried that meds only treated one symptom and created fifteen new ones.

You said I pulled a knife on someone.

I said maybe metaphorically. I asked when that happened, and you said at group therapy. I still do not understand this story. I asked if there were any more notes about that, and you said no. I asked where the knife was, because if I pulled a knife on someone in a psych facility, wouldn't there be evidence? Wouldn't I have been restrained? Why didn't you have answers for any of those questions?

To my twelve white roommates:

Thanks to those of you that visited me, who brought me clothes and pizza.

To my cousin:

Thank you for saying I love you in the blackest way, which is to say, in defiance of the trauma this place caused you, braiding my hair and re-telling Dave Chappelle jokes to make me laugh.

To B & G:

Thank you for driving up every weekend from Providence to see me. My mom and brother were closer geographically and didn't come up once. My brother didn't even call.

To B's Omi:

Thank you for coming to my house the day after Easter to check on me, for showing me the photos in your purse, for telling me about how the Nazis took your father, for letting me know that grief is immortal with your tears. Thank you for bringing me candy and clean underwear the first day I was allowed visitors. You are still the only person I know who could have come into that place and told me, "They feed you, you have a bed, it's not so bad," and that I did not belong where I was.

To Northeastern University:

When I went to email one of my professors, after asking for a week to contact someone to let them know where I was, the hospital social worker assigned to my case fell asleep at her desk. You were asleep the whole time. I still can't grasp how you revoked my teaching assistant-ship, even though I came back with documentation and I explained that I could not afford to continue grad school without it. I had already gotten a stern talking to for trying to balance activism and education. If I were white, I don't think you would have done this. If I had been in a car accident or had cancer, I know you would not have done this. I'm still not sure it was legal, but chose not to fight you because I have never had money to pay for a lawyer, and I'm sure your Raytheon funding would have protected you either way. I am grateful not to have one of your diplomas.

To the Genius Bar employee who attempted to un-brick my phone:

I am still in shock. It was maybe two weeks after I was released. You probably don't remember, but you spent twenty to thirty minutes trying to fix it, and threw up your hands and told me the only possible reason it was in the state it was in was that too many people had been trying to hack into it at the same time.

To my roommates:

I told y'all the feds were watching.

To Depakote:

Thank you for slowing my thought pattern some, but why'd you go flatten my eyes and dehydrate my body to crocodile?

To the hospital psychiatrist:

Isn't there supposed to be a weaning for this? I asked my PCP if she could help with the side effects, and when she called you, you just said to tell me to stop taking it. Pretty sure that's dangerous, but what do I know? I'm just a crazy, invisible-knife-wielding blackgirl, not a doctor.

To my therapist in New York:

I miss you. I was so wary at first, but the day I laid this whole story out, you said it sounded like I was set up. I cried the whole train ride home because I was so overwhelmed by you saying the thing I couldn't speak, because I knew people would just tell me I was paranoid, pat me on the head, and ask me questions that were really just statements about how they didn't trust me.

To all my QTPOC who struggle with mental health issues, which is to say most of us, because the multitude of oppressive systems we face would rather that we disappear than thrive:

I love you. Take care of yourself. Let yourself be taken care of. You deserve love. You deserve care. These words are not enough, can never be enough. You are not invisible. You are not a problem. You are not your illness.

You are. You be. We gon be alright.

May you find your kin. May they hold it down and keep you safe. May we find new roads to healing.

To Casey:

None of that should have happened. I'm sorry for not forgiving you sooner, for allowing anyone who did not love you to get close enough to think they could make your decisions.

I know your whole gorgeous, finally-stable future was right there in front of you when the table got flipped over. I know you wanted to die for the first time in your life when you got home but never considered suicide. You're stubborn in that way. It's almost confusing.

Brute force alone isn't healing. Remember that. Some days you are going to be a brick in your own windshield. Some days you will feel as golden as you want to be. No days are wrong.

You're still here. You deserve security.

Hold fast to every act of love you've been granted and don't let go. It won't always be enough, but you are lucky to have the support you do. Don't forget it's there. Don't forget yourself.

FUTURESEX

I'll fuck the ocean in broad daylight.
My gender is somewhere between 1996 Lil' Kim
and 2075 maple tree I planted in third grade.
I won't open my legs for less than
it costs to love every inch of me.
Most days I'll stick my cock into eager men,
or the sky anyhow. My tongue is still short
and hungry, but never thirsty. I have many
lovers—bookcases, fainting couches, cellos,
mostly furniture, although occasionally
concepts like a public option or memory.
I don't fuck everything I love, same as now.
I love everything I fuck, even me, which is new.
My gender is a murmuration of starlings.
My sexuality is a chainsaw made of lavender.
Neither is the most important thing about me,
not nearly as important as the way I feel about them.
All my exes live in Siberia and I can't remember
anything but the ducklings they saved from traffic.

Nobody cares who you sleep with, or how many.
No body is socially deemed sexier than any other,
except Prince's. Just deal with it.

Growing up, kids play the dozens like:
Yo mama so fat, and nobody cares.
Yo daddy rocks a pencil skirt meaner than the President.
Yo parent so logical they like Spock, sun.
Yo mama so fine she look like Prince.
Yo shame so puny it's fun-sized.
Yo shame so nah it's invisible.
Yo fear so ha! sex ed teaches abstinence from it.

I'm 120 and I'm going fuck the ocean like an oxygen mask
in broad daylight with all my life's genders,

with all my little loves, my biggest one, myself,
with all the sun's might, and it's not how I die,
it's how I live from day to day, forgetting
how cumbersome it was to live without joy.

For those still living

It should not be a burden to breathe, and yet...
some days the down trod,
the overdraft fees,
the simple drag of getting out of bed,
yes, we all know,
so please, open the flood gates
and let oxygen pour life back in.

Lovers leave & money & sometimes whole lives,
but here we are, together.

Consider the mother of seven,
left with four,
one in the cradle
one bullet hole in the neighbor's floorboards
a heart attack after the kidney took,
and a husband passed there too.
Consider my grandmother,
dark eyes that constantly look wet,
fixed on the Sox game,
trying to look away from what's coming
for all of us.

Or the 18-year-old refugee,
Congo to Nigeria to South Dakota.
Imagine the running in her blood.
Safety taunts her like a schoolyard bully,
and the first sunlight cracks open over her
every morning like gunfire, but
there, look, the movement of the lungs,
a hand on her shoulder that wishes
it was an embryo of healing.

We all survive something
if we're still here.
I don't like to use the word miracle,
but our language affords us little else
for the pushing that happens between
birth and obstacle after obstacle after...
sometimes it is easy to forget
that our bodies are the spastic
joyous noise of sunshine.

When the suicide note goes to the mortgage company
and Tuesday morning finds the train cars filled with women
in tears at the headlines, the grimace glides in
from all the dark crevices in our marrow
but let us not forget the movement which propels us
and cease to condemn our own velocities.

It would be to simple to stuff
fear like hay into shirt sacks.
Scarecrows without mind enough
to understand how belief is built
into each and every one of us.

In what rubs the nerve endings raw
and the soft patter of infinite molecules.
The fingernail tapping at the glass
of your pulse, it's happening.

If we did not believe that we were
congregated and passing
carbon dioxide amongst us,
we would be awash on the rocks of
a sunless place, alone.

Sometimes we've felt this way,
the dismal sound of bile in our bellies,
head empty of all else but ugly
confusion and I know
that some of us have been to the edges,

but now, make a noise, any noise.
and here, know that you are present
and accounted for.

Consider this a sermon,
and you're the choir,
and you look great!

Your fingers are singing!
And your eyelashes!
And your voices, please,
lend them to a simple song,
don't be bashful.
Scarecrows and slipper keepers
let us breathe
together.

BEINGS OF SOUND

When I was told that the word person means "being of sound," it made me think of the dull crash of water my mother made when she dove into the pool fully clothed to save me from drowning when I was three.

It made me think of flatlines, traffic, clacking heels, sex, spoons in teacups, church, fryolators, guns, apples, chalkboards, faucets, typewriters, firecrackers, double dutch, snorting coke, helicopters, pool tables, ringtones, matches, John Cage in a soundless room listening to his own heartbeat, and scenes of bodies falling:

Chris hit the bathroom floor loud enough for his mother to hear and come running to find him dead from heroin again, revived from ambulances again, a week before Christmas. His mouth vacuumed air at bullet speed and it sounded like "Silver Bells." He tells me about it later, casual as a convenience store.

Uncle David dropped to the pavement scratching his face against the tarmac with the click and jangle of handcuffs. Policemen will help your body fall if you don't want to let it. Policemen's bodies fall into bed at night, fall in the line of duty, fall but never noiseless. We all do.

One time I fell from a hammock in Nicaragua because a feral dog pushed me. It was pretty funny. Sand doesn't make much noise. Coconuts hitting tin roofs do. There was a man named George Washington there. He wasn't that George Washington. He wanted to dance. His hands were rough from years of fishing with just the line and no pole. He said, "You can't waste music," like some day we're going to run out of it. It was slow calypso, and you could hear our sweat in it.

Someone once told me that the word person broken down meant "being of sound." It could have been a book, but I swear I heard it rattle and fire neurons. It made me think of clacking sex, chalk matches, zippers, snorting double dutch, guncopters, cokeolaytors, church in teacups, typecrackers, traffic heels, John Cage in a soundless room listening to brainwaves and thinking of all the words that sound good together but don't have any meaning yet. Like unborn languages.

It made me think of languageseeds that grow symbols every time the bass beat from a car stereo leaks under the sidewalk. It made me think that the earth's core is a bass beat humming upwards using cars for a voice. It made me think that we are all falling bodies dropped from some unknown winged thing made of cellos and turntables and harps and speeches falling down into each other. We are bodies of sound pulling our children out of prison and gasping, resuscitated and grabbing at oxygen like it was handcuffed to our children. We are beings of sound and sometimes when we fall down it looks like dancing because our brainwaves are bass beats.

When George Washington told me, "you can't waste music," he meant the sound of being was too precious to be wasted falling in killing fields, and that if we aren't dancing now, then when will we?

WHOSE CLOCK?

KUEBIKO

Standing watch over a field of boneroot
in bellowing silence, the straw man
will say there is nothing to be done
while chapels burn across the horizon.

At dawn the tractor roars in hot pursuit
of the rabbits, planting shotgun shells
for next year's harvest, and the drunk
farmer mows two children, but scared

crow is immobile. They sent him
to the field to report on invasive species
brought here from the Old World—
bloodleaf, deadnettle, gunpowder.

Eventually he was crucified,
damned to the frozen post,
and all that was left to do
was hum the old tune

If I only had a...

CASSANDRA CLOWNS LADY TIRESIAS

Your pussy so temporary it came with 7-Year Vagisil.
Your bloodline so weak, nan one birth by decapitation.
Ya mama so basic she couldn't save you
                    from her own goddess.
Ya mama so basic she accepted your visions
                              like that was some kinda gift.

You know how I got this curse?
Apollo spit in my mouth
for telling him no.

Your lookin ass, peeping in Mount Olympus windows
got ole swole foot Eddie tryna get like you,
cuz you told him he a muhfucker, f'real.

They listen to you even though
the number of people dead on your watch
higher than Suge Knight's body count.

I ran for that wooden nag at the gates
            bout to clap first, cuz I stay
            woker than all y'all.

When they sacked the city, the only thanks I got
was hands laid on me by some savage lesser—now
I don't care whose star player he was,
if the goon's too scared to collect him in church
muhfucker will catch that fire sooner
                              or late.

These people only remember me
clinging to a statue,
a pretty-but-crazy bitch.
Their vases come for me like
like they finna put out
the sunshine between my legs.

Now soothsay me this—
what you ever foretold
a woman that she ain't known
                    her whole life?

LOVING U IS COMPLICATED

because u gather me up in ur lap and tell me u're jealous of my grey hairs after spending the whole morning stewing over the girl u left in LA who lied about where the money went.

∞

because u expect me to cook and tell me to eat less while u eat my house brick by brick without ever tasting this wet, but u cram ur flagpole down my throat any chance u get.

∞

because every girlfriend u've ever had is white. because I am barely an exception. because I would placate ur Nana if u brought me back home. because u still fucked a "reformed" neo-Nazi after she told u her husband was in jail for near-murdering a black man because u thought her Chelsea haircut was cute.

∞

because after I fought that white man off me u took me to the clinic and then put enough distance between us to fit a national border.

∞

because u tell me sexism doesn't exist, that *girls feeling bad about themselves isn't as bad as young brothers wrecking their bodies tryna make it pro* OR u talk endlessly about the plight of the black woman but got someone else to tell me I should read one passage from Fanon as a balm for the day u equated my being raped to a poem I wrote about u.

∞

because we made lemonade and u asked if I wanted kids on our first date, and said u liked it when I drooled on your shoulder in my sleep.

∞

because u vast. because u contain kin.

∞

because I call u every year on yr birthday and u act like that minute is a burden, and u don't call me on mine, or when I get locked up in a psych ward, only call me if somebody dies or u need me to staunch our mother's weeping. because u were so drunk I took ur keys and u tried to fight me on the bar patio & u don't remember my gorgeous full court three-pointer landing them in the parking lot.

∞

because u sold coke and worked for the post office and still didn't pay child support. Because u don't believe Auntie when she tells u she caught ur father in bed with ur now dead sister. because u hard pressed to believe ur sisters unless they kicking the stitches in ur stomach open.

∞

because it was always revolution or art or money or sex over love. because u killed urself or someone else, or tried to and failed. because u are my best friend, first kiss, favorite teacher, day healer, night crooner, hand on my smallest back, knife to my broadest chest, second opinion, brother: blood and play, father: absent or dead.
because u can't even
see me

                                        until I'm taking aim.

LOWER NINTH, APRIL 2006

I. "Bad Moon Rising" came on the radio
           on the Pontchartrain Causeway Bridge.

The orange X's and the tally
           of bodies, *TFW* a blood hex
                      that says do not cross this threshold
                                 without a triage of masks.

We unraveled our sleeping bags
           in a third-floor classroom at St. Mary of the Angels,
                      Yankees come South unsure how else
                                 to help the living rebuild.

On the chalkboard, a survivor's message:
           We stayed for three days, waiting for the Coast Guard and when they
                      flew over they ignored us.
           When we ran out of food and water, we had to go.
           They left us here to die.
           RIP Trayvaughn, Yana SJ, Big Eric, Lil Susie, Mikey,
                      Trice Lumumba, OG Fred, Victor, Gracie, Sandy B,
                                 Air Jordan, Jr King, Mere Rice, Mr. Evers,
                                            Cyn, The Reverend Doctor, Rennie Ma

I spent the week hitting bathroom tiles with a sledgehammer,
or trying to salvage photo albums and school books.
The Red Cross tried to feed us hot dogs as if it was our block
while we were eating po boys and drinking Red Stripe on a stoop.

Packs of dogs gone feral patrolled the unlit
parking lots, and plenty of locals would tell you
how they heard the government detonated the levee.

II. On the third day, new white folks arrived and unrolled their bags.
    Two pony-tailed girls read the chalkboard and called it a lie.
    A circle of ghosts sucked their teeth.

When they took erasers to the board,
I wanted to tackle them but froze in disbelief
    at the haywire minds of savages,
    their insistence upon looking dead
    into our ineffable faces
    and treating
    our many deaths
    as our biggest deceptions
    and our only proper attire.

The Universe as Seen Through a Keyhole
(after Eduardo Galeano)

In the fall a young Bengali boy play-fought with an elderly Polish man in the man's yard, the boy pretended to steal the man's bike, and they laughed knowing it was all in fun. In the evenings, the old man played the accordion in time to the call to prayer coming from the mosque. The leaves gathered at the feet of the sound, a captive audience.

On the first day of winter a vandal smashed the old man's windows. The next day as he and his friend cut the wood to board up the windows, smoke billowed from the attic of the squat next door where an Irish woman who looked much older than she was lived. The boy watched the firefighters with other boys from the end of the street, hypnotized by the bombastic water or the crackling heat or the snapping door frame. The man watched, too, with his friends from his yard.

When spring arrived, the boy began to play soccer in the lot across from the old man's house with other boys about his age. The old man played the accordion, though you could no longer hear his music from the street. Even as it got warmer, snow kept coming down and the leaves continued to fall like ash.

AGE AIN'T NOTHIN BUT A NUMBER

When she was princess of the damned,
the marriage certificate went public,
and like all honeymoons it ended
in a cemetery of deflated balloons.
No one gifted the couple a pitchfork.
She switched labels, and the annulment
got swept under the rug like the names
of all the girls he had poached from
the Southside after the dismissal bell.

In the summer of 1998 my second cousin
kissed me without tongue, just the red peck
of tension. Later on in his mom's rented
beach house, he cuddled up beside me,
put his foot on top of mine. The adults
remarked how cute it was, how innocent.
It was a blushing thing, to be wanted
and impossible—the gold standard of
being a thirteen-year-old girl.

That summer she was the only thing on the radio,
slate leather and side bang, gladiator crop top—
the effortless falconer training all the mallrat
denizens of Wet Seal how to swoop, dip low,
slip past the grown men reaching for our hips.

When 300,000 of any species disappear
they are named endangered, except
for black girls. The quiet hush of stardom
allowed him to press their backs into cotton
like notary stamps on the wet mud.

Who could say she wasn't starstruck too,
that she wasn't lost before we airbrushed
her on every surface of the sky? The lean
of her cool, a casket to broadcast, and
another earthen hole to fill with absence.

Epigenetics

I am every kind of threat.
High-pink code red.

Auntie B is my biological father's
ambassador to my psych-ward knifedom.
She brings   her grandkids,
eyes sweet with fear   over
having another grown-folks mess
　　　　seeding their dreams.

The horizon is a rusted sickle, iron sky reflected salt flat and billowing
　　like a portal trying to shudder its eyes.　In the parking lot B let slip
　　she was once prisoner to the ward, and maybe this is where birds are born
　　　　　　　　　　and where we die,　in　　　　a castle made of piss
　　　　　　　　　　　　buckets　　moat　　　　　　drawbridge
　　　　　　　　　　　　　　paved　with
　　　　　　　　　　　　　glittering psychotropic　　　　bricks
　　　　　　　　　　　　　crow's nest　　　shock　　　　　no
　　　　　　　　　　　　　　　　wind

The kids need to use the visitor restroom and B
        snatches the clock's wig the moment they leave.

                Are you ashamed of the family?
                Is that why you don't keep in touch?

                        Isn't it you who made the sand glass?

When were you here before? Not your daughter
        hauled up from the mudflats after a dreamemory
            of an undulating spider of calloused hands in   and   B's
omissions.

                                What did it to *you* Auntie?

                If you want to play chicken   the lithium is
                    starting to kick   and bet
                    I   won't   remember   to   blink.

Guitar Bains Interviews Kanye West

Why you putting that shit up your nose?

                You can't tell me…

Look, cuz, they're still killing us
and you out here like you forgot
about Ollie North even tho you named
your babygirl after him,
and you in the studio pushing this
lacefront Freeway Ricky to be grimier
than the fact he used to be a CO.

                            nothing.

Alright then, let's talk about that one line
about leaving dat ass for a white girl.

                Nah, see. You're not gon talk about my girl
                when you think revolution means no pussy
                or Hen? I been doing this more than you.

Brother, you want to be me but you Milk,
toast, it's a rap. Everybody want a black man's life
except you. You wanna play at being a seamstress?
Fine, go stitch up every bullet hole in South Side.

                You ain't got the answers. Out here
                hunting your Day One and all you got
                to show is raggedy peacock feathers &
                blood on your sleeves. That's coon shit.
                You can't tell me nothing. You ain't my mirror.

You're right. I'm your grandfather
clock counting the Black Skkknhead
beat. You marching to *my* rhythm.
If it's my life you want, then c'mon.

BEGGAR'S BANQUET

Let's talk about our parents' teeth,
the way they slip from their mouths
and take months to grow back ceramic
or never grow back at all,
the way we watch them spit out mid-sentence
and jammed back into soft, rotten gums
like fingernails into bars of soap.

Let's talk about their exhausted bodies,
our exhausted bodies, my father
laying on the couch for thirty minutes after work,
how I would play the inherited family piano
with untrained hands until he drifted off,
how I would stop and he would tell me
to keep playing when I thought he was asleep,
how my mom had to sell the piano after he died
in order to make mortgage payments, how that
didn't stop the impending foreclosure.

Let's talk about all of the stab wounds
we try to staunch with our mouths,
or stitches we pull open with our teeth
in order to be seen in this world that despises
our worn shoes and crass tongues
but wants to lick our stories clean from our plates
in order to tell them their way,
tell us what we deserve.

Let's convene in the great hall,
lift glasses full of our shared tears,
and let our alienation rest for just
a short while as we look each other
in the eye in the ballroom where
we will never belong. Let's waltz
just to know that we are not alone
even though the chandeliers exist
and the glasses are made of crystal
and our parents will come and
vacuum the carpet after we go home.

What Work Does

Dad drove me to the Chamber of Commerce
in what used to be Stephen's Ford Escort.
We never talked about his dialysis
or the wake of bodies.
He just played Stevie Wonder's "As"
on the tape player even though
he normally listened to classic rock.

He said he was happy
I stopped working as a grill cook
and found an office job,
that I was too smart
to be working with food.

A month after the transplant,
I started my senior year of high school
and he returned to Star Market.

He had a heart attack in his sleep
after a week on his feet.

We could have blamed the doctors,

or the fresh kidney that should have
granted him another forty years.

Or God,

but the hospital bills
and the unpaid leave,
and his restless hands, eager
to chuck bruised fruit again…

His headstone bears a cornucopia.
His killer remains at large.

HEARTS FROM GOLD

My uncle killed himself
          nine years after the kidney
my dad gifted him wouldn't take.
          They kept him at the bottom
of the donation list
          with one foot in the grave, he'd say,
before it was both,
          before he turned to blue ash,
at 44.

∞

When they opened David Rockefeller
          to gift him his sixth shiny new heart
wrinkled pearls and heat lightning fell out.

At 99, he still used death to avoid itself,
          found the fountain of youth

in corpse after corpse after corpse after corpse after corpse after corpse

like money could bribe the reaper forever,
like his best years were still ahead of him.

Topsy (current)

You are an aggregate—rachetqueen and exile and first lady—
Nowhere citizen, though you birthed humanity, and it suckles
every liter of your cultures, your gross domestic products.
When they say we used to be kings and queens, not all of us.
Why so wistful? All kingdoms have peasants at the ready.

You are an aggregate—blood, rosewater, ambrosia—
You sprung forth from head of Harriet's shotgun.
Named in amphibrach, spondee, sometimes resumé,
naming yourself, never born, growing wild. You
will answer to nothing outside that circle of grain.

You are mixed so the hims call you beautiful,
and ain't that about as rotten inside as muleshit?
You are the hymns we sing to uplift us, gorgeous
from night sky to fading star. It's you who told hims
how they matter, how hymns are just matter, too.

You are a combine—tobacco, cotton, sugar cane—
and if the world's d boys were a nation they'd be G20,
mules are middle management, and trap queens CEOs.
You are the harvest, your own electric bounty, maybe
your mother's gardens, always a feast of earth and sun.

You are a composite sketch of a matriarch parade,
the kind of love that shouts down boulevards. If they
only wants a taste, tell them close their mouths. You
are never too much except your mercy. The heart wants
what the brain thinks it deserves. What's it say?

You meld worlds to save yourself, how wicked. You witch, burning
books that renamed you Billie after your blueprint and sorrowed
mornings. Strung out, dizzy, she looked Etta in the eye and said
this will be you. All your love is blue
and cold in flames. All your love is a savior you did not expect.

114

You are an aggregate—Pangea and library and Big Bang—
A stampede, all tusk and recognition. You contain multitudes,
and not a one is uglier than the speculation on your body
from birth. Dust yourself off, turn your pages, find the passage
where your heart wants your own best you, and wail.

It wants you. It wants you. It wants you.

THE DOZEN

About the Poet

Casey Rocheteau was born on Cape Cod and raised as a sea witch. She was the recipient of the inaugural Write A House permanent residency in Detroit in 2014. She has attended Callaloo Writer's Workshop, Cave Canem, and Bread Loaf Writers' Conference in Sicily. She is an Artist in Residence at InsideOut Literary Arts in Detroit and an editor at *The Offing*.

About the Cover Artist

Vanessa Reynolds is a Detroit-based creative. She is a professional tattoo artist who is also lead vocalist and guitarist for the Detroit band RiverSpirit. Musical works by Vanessa can be found at river-spirit.com.

About the Press

Sibling Rivalry Press is an independent press based in Little Rock, Arkansas. Its mission is to publish work that disturbs and enraptures. This book was published in part due to the support of the Sibling Rivalry Press Foundation, a non-profit private foundation dedicated to assisting small presses and small press authors.

CPSIA information can be obtained at www.ICGtesting.com
Printed in the USA
BVOW08s0640020716

454324BV00003B/7/P